FIDDLE TUNES FOR FLATPICKERS
MANDOLIN

BY BOB GRANT

PLAYBACK+

Speed • Pitch • Balance • Loop

To access audio visit:
www.halleonard.com/mylibrary

4990-8161-3397-8525

ISBN 978-0-8256-8753-2

HAL•LEONARD®

Visit Hal Leonard Online at
www.halleonard.com

Contact us:
Hal Leonard
7777 West Bluemound Road
Milwaukee, WI 53213
Email: info@halleonard.com

In Europe, contact:
Hal Leonard Europe Limited
42 Wigmore Street
Marylebone, London, W1U 2RN
Email: info@halleonardeurope.com

In Australia, contact:
Hal Leonard Australia Pty. Ltd.
4 Lentara Court
Cheltenham, Victoria, 3192 Australia
Email: info@halleonard.com.au

Acknowledgments
Thanks to my many students, who have inspired me to pick apart
what I do unconsciously and demand that I explain it clearly—it
has made me a better player and a special thank you to
Tonya Upchurch for putting up with me.

Steven Berryessa, for whom most of these transcriptions where written out for.

TABLE OF CONTENTS

PREFACE

The mandolin and the fiddle have a lot in common. Both instruments are tuned the same, share the same register, and are roughly the same scale (size), so it's only natural that the tunes played on one can be easily adapted to be played on the other.

American fiddling traces its origins to the British Islands, where most of the immigrants in eighteenth-century Appalachia were from. These tunes were handed down through the years until they took on a distinctly American style.

Naturally, other tunes were written in this style, and a tradition of fiddling was developed through the folk process. This book contains songs that are anywhere from a couple of hundred years old to the more recently penned tunes by Bill Monroe.

AUDIO TRACK LIST

1. Old Joe Clark
2. Old Joe Clark (Alternate B Section)
3. Salt Creek
4. Sally Goodin'
5. Bill Cheatham
6. Cherokee Shuffle
7. Fire on the Mountain
8. Sweet Liza Jane
9. Devil's Dream
10. Red Haired Boy
11. Big Mon
12. Old Dangerfield
13. Cattle in the Cane
14. Cluck Old Hen
15. Texas Gales
16. Billy in the Low Ground
17. Boston Boy
18. Sailor's Hornpipe
19. Whiskey Before Breakfast
20. Soldier's Joy
21. Eighth of January
22. Liberty
23. Liberty (Alternate A Section)
24. Fisher's Hornpipe
25. Arkansas Traveler
26. Blackberry Blossom
27. Temperance Reel
28. Turkey in the Straw
29. Kentucky Mandolin

INTRODUCTION

This book was designed to help beginning to advanced mandolin players build a repertoire of commonly played fiddle tunes.

Since most of these traditional tunes have been passed around from musician to musician (in some cases over hundreds of years) and have gradually been changed by the musicians who play them, the versions presented here are interpretations rather than exact melodies.

While the melody of the tunes is emphasized in these arrangements, they will frequently include variations on the theme, interesting ornamentations, or alternate parts.

As you learn these tunes, you will recognize and learn different techniques used in certain situations such as slides, double stops, fiddle shuffles, tremolos, double-time ornaments, and syncopations. Once you learn these techniques, you will be able to apply them to other songs.

HOW TO USE THIS BOOK

Each tune in this book presents a new challange. To help you, a brief explanation of the challenging passages, fingerings, positions, or trouble spots precedes every song.

The accompanying audio has a demonstration track for each example. The audio allows you to hear the mandolin alone or the accompaniment without the mandolin by just panning the balance control on your stereo all the way left (accompaniment) or right (mandolin).

After learning the tunes, get them up to speed so that you can practice along with the audio tracks—this will prepare you for playing with a group.

Earl Scruggs

TABLATURE

Every tune is presented in standard notation and *tablature*, which eliminates any ambiguities that might go into what fingering might be best for a specific passage or phrase.

Tablature (TAB) is music notation shorthand for stringed instruments and is very easy to read. The four horizontal lines represent the four doubled strings of the mandolin, from high to low. The number indicates the fret and the line tells you which string to press down. It's similar to reading chord diagrams but sideways.

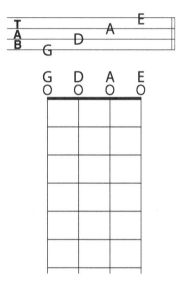

Common Tablature Symbols

Hammer-On
Pick the indicated string, then sound an upper note by hammering on to the string with the finger.

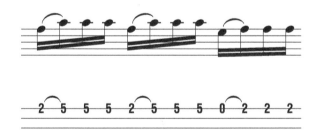

Pull-off
Finger two notes on the same string. Then pick the upper note and sound the lower note by plucking the string with the fretting finger.

Slide
Play the first note normally, then slide the left-hand finger to the second note. A slide line connects the notes of a slide. When a slide line comes from no other note (as in many cases in the following arrangements), slide up or down from a point a few frets above or below the note.

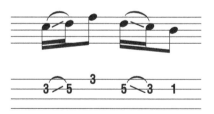

READING MUSIC

The next thing you need to be able to do is to apply rhythm to the numbers on the TAB lines. To achieve this, you will have to look at the standard notation staff above the TAB.

At the beginning of the song you will see the *time signature*. The top number tells you how many beats are in a measure and the bottom number tells you what note gets the beat:

There are five rhythmic values that you are going to need to know: whole notes, half notes, quarter notes, eighth notes, and sixteenth notes.

If the time signature is ⁴⁄₄ it means that a *quarter note* gets *one* beat. Therefore, a *whole note* will get *four* beats, and a *half note* will last *two* beats. Each quarter note can also be divided into *two eighth notes*, or *four sixteenth notes*.

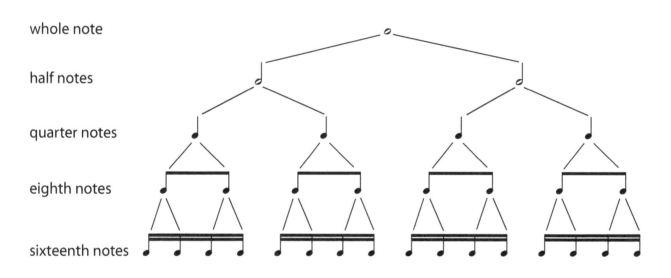

A note's rhythm is identified by the flag attached to its stem.

eighth notes

sixteenth notes

Consecutive eighth or sixteenth notes can be *beamed* together.

beamed eighth notes

beamed sixteenth notes

Proper picking technique is essential when playing fiddle tunes. You have to move your pick in the right direction to achieve the right sense of power and dynamics that each song requires. The following patterns will help you achieve the proper picking technique.

Down-Up Pattern

Let's take a look at a group of four sixteenth notes (one beat). The first and third notes are strong beats (also called *downbeats*) and would be picked with *downstrokes,* represented by ⊓ (down); the second and fourth notes are weak beats (also called *upbeats*) and would be picked with *upstrokes,* represented by ∨ (up). This creates a consistent *down-up-down-up* (DUDU) pattern.

Down-Down-Up Pattern

In the following example, the pick directions stay the same. You are just removing the second note of the pattern but keeping the pick direction intact. This is a *down-down-up* pattern (DDU).

Down-Up-Down Pattern

Remove the fourth note and you will get a *down-up-down* pattern (DUD).

Down-Up-Up Pattern

Remove the third note and you have a *down-up-up* pattern (DUU). This pattern never changes—no exceptions—it creates a strict alternate picking style that provides the power and volume that you'll need for playing an acoustic instrument such as the mandolin. If you break this pattern everything that comes after will sound rough and clumsy.

THE TUNES—KEY OF A

Old Joe Clark is a favorite at fiddle contests and Bluegrass festivals across the country. Although this is a fairly straight version of the tune, be careful with the slide up into the unison notes.

These slides should be played as fast as grace notes, almost simultaneously.

OLD JOE CLARK

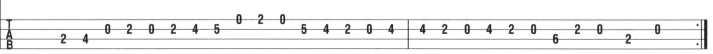

This tune is also known as "Salt River," and is one of the most played fiddle tunes. As mentioned earlier, watch out for the slides in the A section but draw them out slightly.

The first and third measures of the B section start with a DUU picking pattern. There is a reverse slide in measures five and six that sounds really cool when played correctly.

SALT CREEK

Track 3

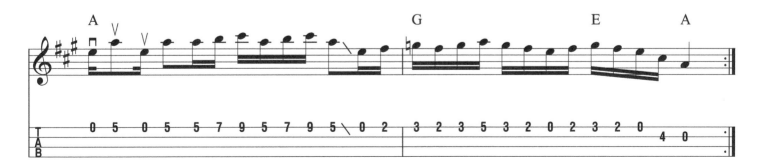

THE TUNES—KEY OF A

The arrangement of this tune is one of the most straightforward reading notations available. The fiddler usually holds down an A (D string, seventh fret) pedal tone while playing the A part, which makes the tune quite challenging.

After you've mastered the tune, try playing it this way.

SALLY GOODIN'

Traditional

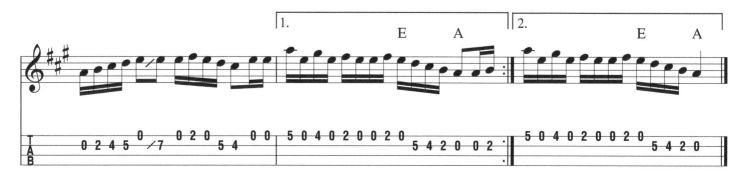

Check out the G natural in the second measure, it gives this tune a bluesy sound.

The B section is made up of lots of arpeggios. Remember to use strict alternate picking and practice very slowly, especially the B section.

BILL CHEATHAM

Traditional

Track 5

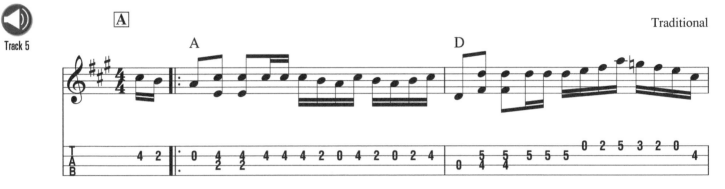

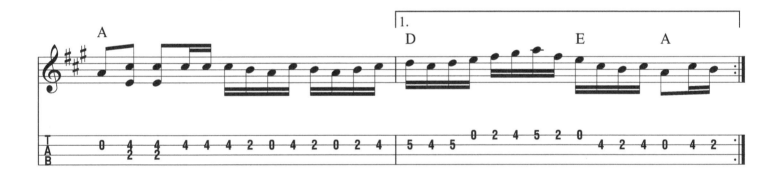

THE TUNES—KEY OF A

Pay special attention to the hammer-ons in the second measure; hit the note cleanly because you need to make the unpicked note as loud as the picked notes.

CHEROKEE SHUFFLE

Traditional

This song is usually played really fast, so there is no time for any fancy stuff—just play it. There are only a few places where you are not playing sixteenth notes; therefore, the picking feels similar to an unbroken sentence.

FIRE ON THE MOUNTAIN

Track 7

Traditional

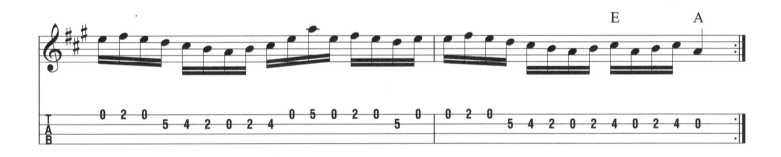

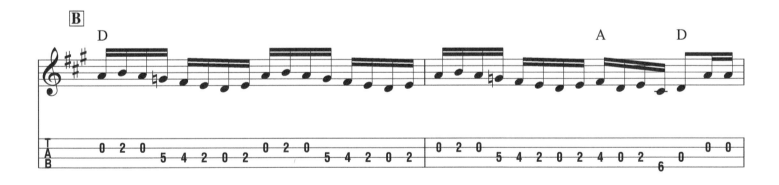

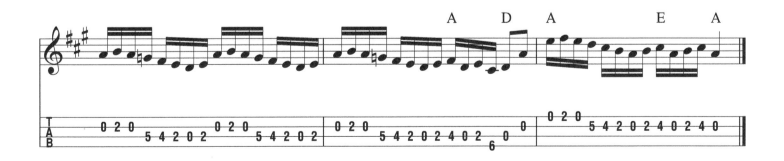

THE TUNES—KEY OF A

The tricky part in this song is where the grace note hammer-ons appear in the A section. Be sure to play them cleanly because they go by pretty fast and can sound sloppy if you are not careful.

SWEET LIZA JANE

Traditional

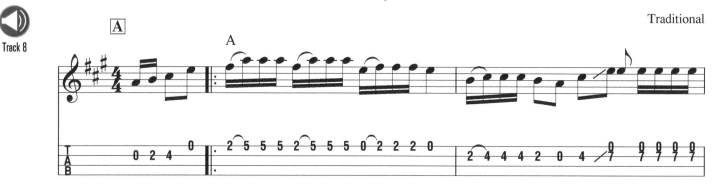

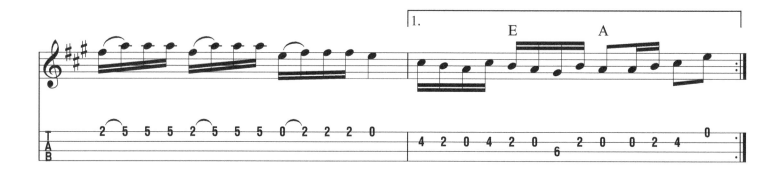

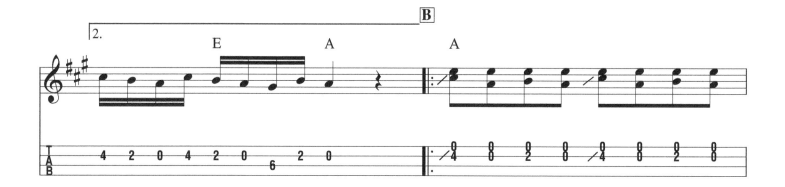

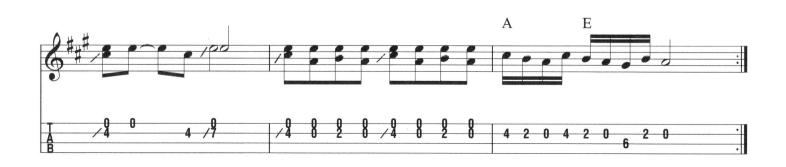

This tune gives the impression that there are two fiddles playing. The key to this song is not playing it too fast—take it easy.

DEVIL'S DREAM

Traditional

Track 9

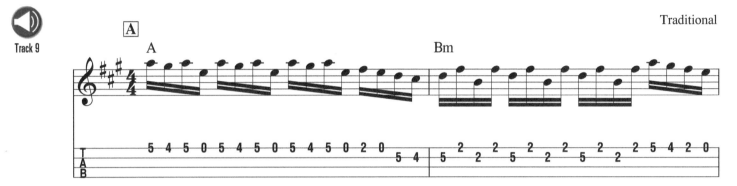

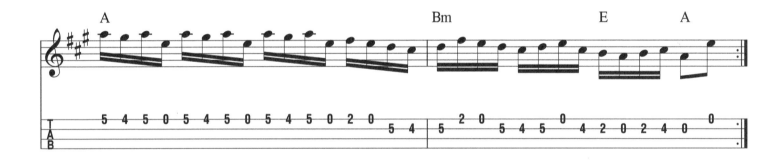

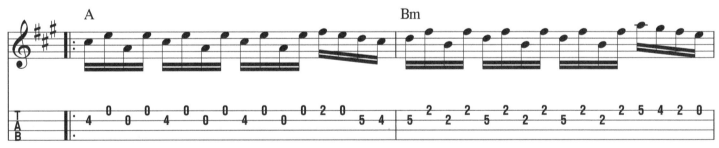

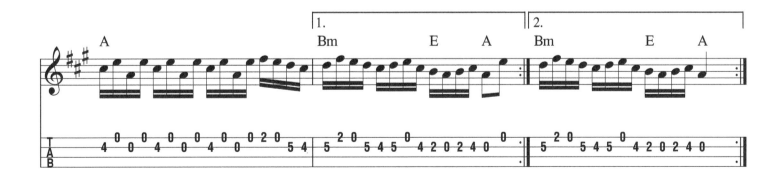

THE TUNES—KEY OF A

This tune has a couple of trouble spots in both left and right hands. There is a sixteenth-note triplet on the last beat of the first measure; pay attention to the pick markings. This same part also has a chromatic run; use your second finger on the C♯ and the third to slide from the D to the D♯.

There is another chromatic run in the second measure, use your third finger on the G and your second finger to slide from the F♯ to the F natural (♮). As before, watch your pick direction.

RED HAIRED BOY

Traditional

This is a classic Bill Monroe tune—a real barnburner. Practice this tune slowly and build up speed gradually.

BIG MON

Track 11

Bill Monroe

THE TUNES—KEY OF A

This is one of the most popular Bill Monroe tunes. It has a cool bend in the first measure that gives the tune a funkier feel. Be careful of the extra beat going into the C section.

OLD DANGERFIELD

Bill Monroe

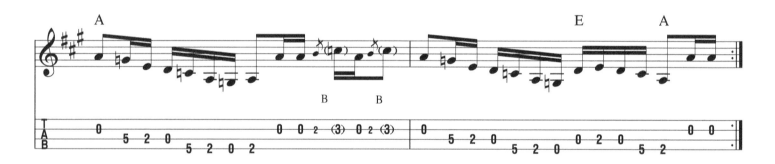

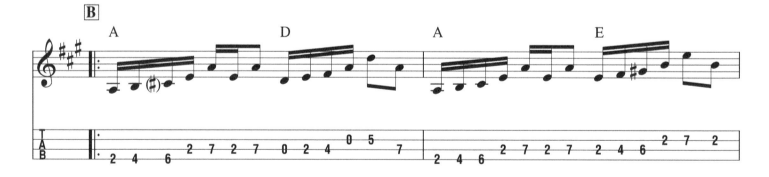

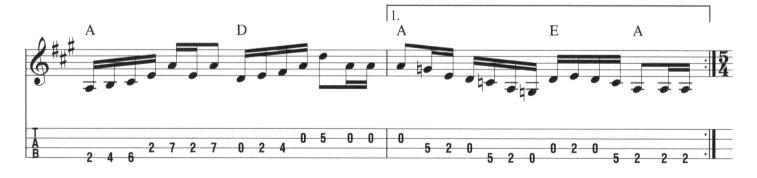

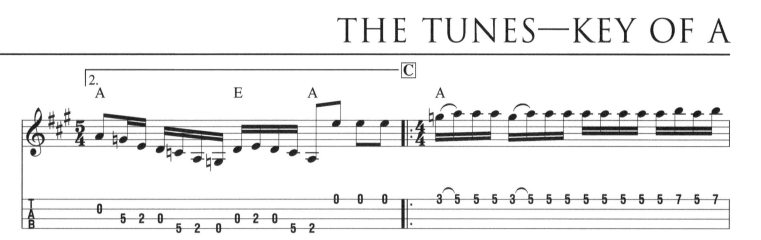

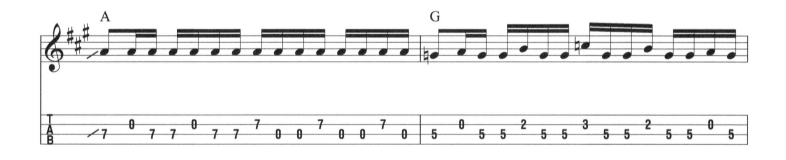

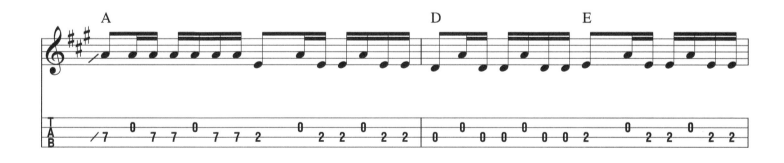

THE TUNES—KEY OF A

This tune is fairly straightforward as far as playing goes—just look out for a couple of slides to the unison.

There is a really cool change from A major to A minor going from the A part to the B part.

CATTLE IN THE CANE

Traditional

Track 13

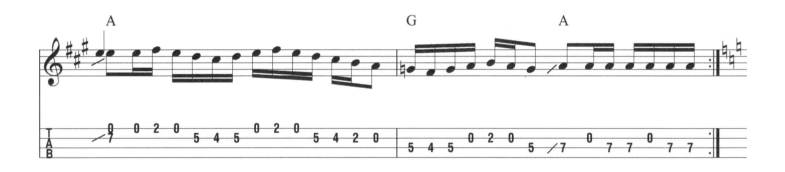

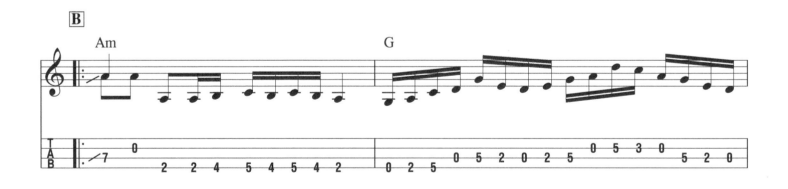

This is an old-fashioned arrangement of this classic tune. The feel is the most important thing when playing this song. Watch out for the double stops in the B part.

CLUCK OLD HEN

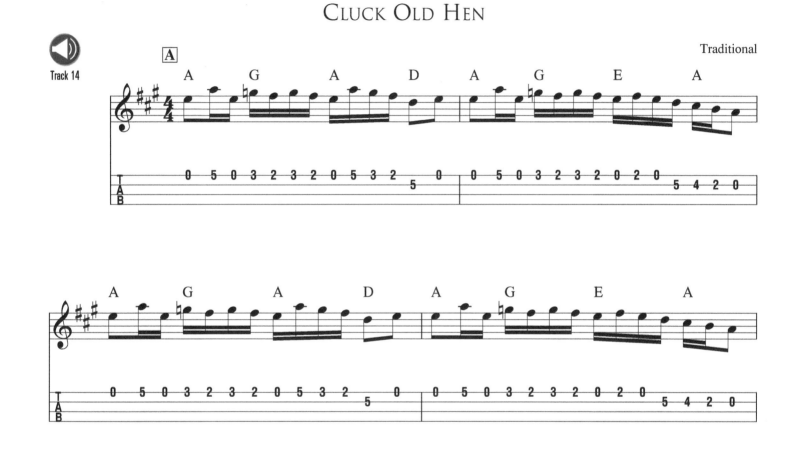

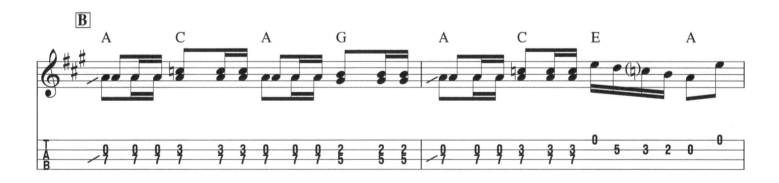

THE TUNES—KEY OF C

The following three tunes share common parts. The B part of "Texas Gales" is also the B part of "Billy in the Low Ground," and its C part is the B part of "Boston Boy."

When you learn "Texas Gales" you will also have learned the B part to both of the other tunes.

TEXAS GALES

Track 15

Traditional

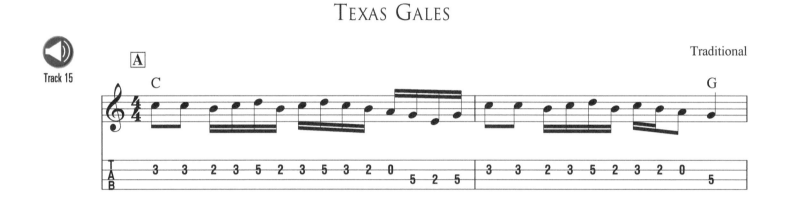

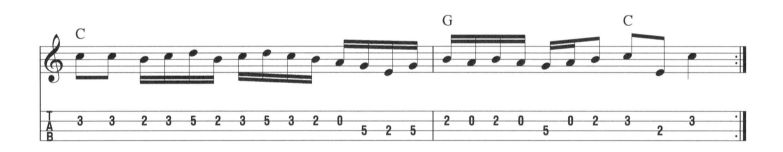

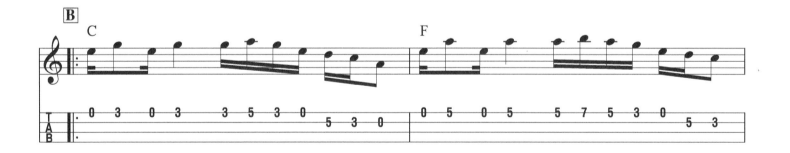

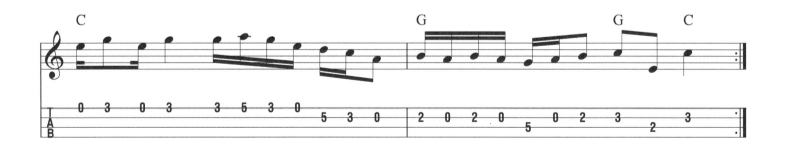

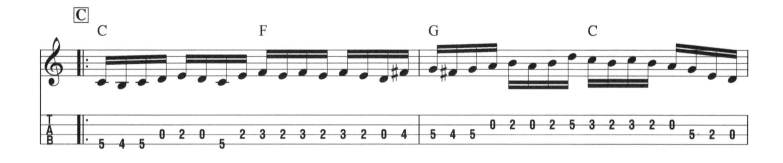

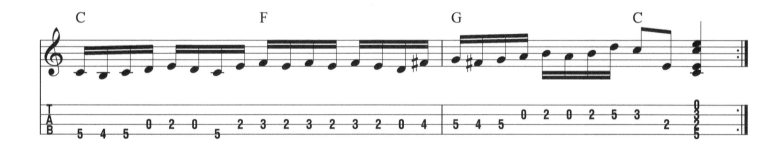

BILLY IN THE LOW GROUND

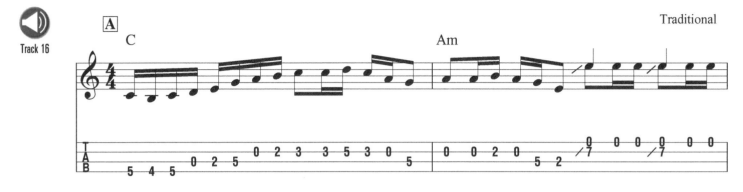

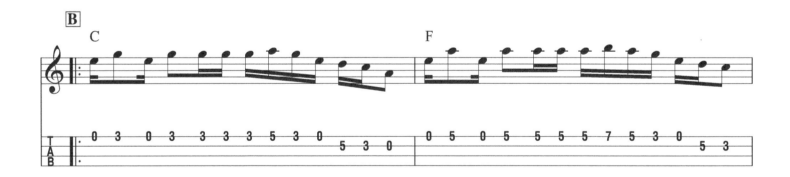

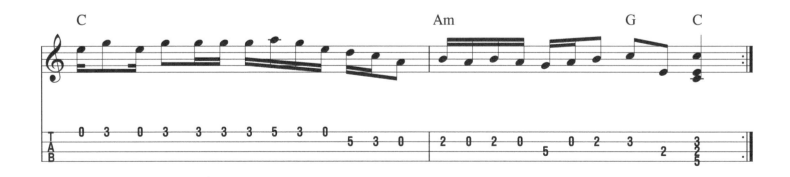

Boston Boy

Traditional

Track 17

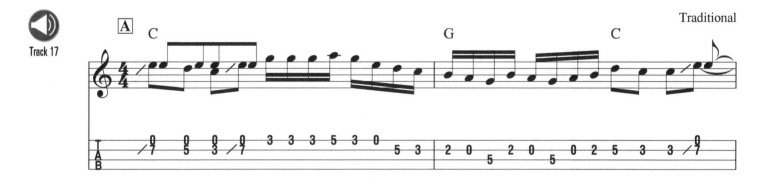

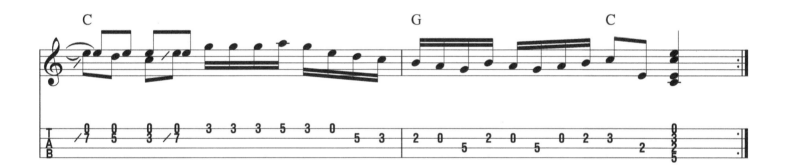

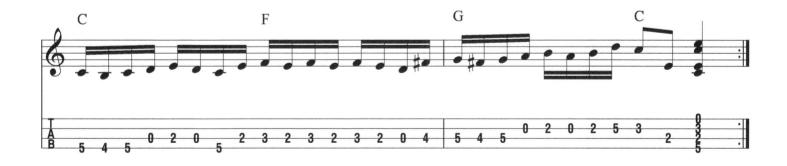

THE TUNES—KEY OF D

Commonly known as the "Popeye theme," no book of fiddle tunes would be complete without this old gem. This song has an interesting mix of leaps, rhythmic variations, and arpeggios.

SAILOR'S HORNPIPE

Traditional

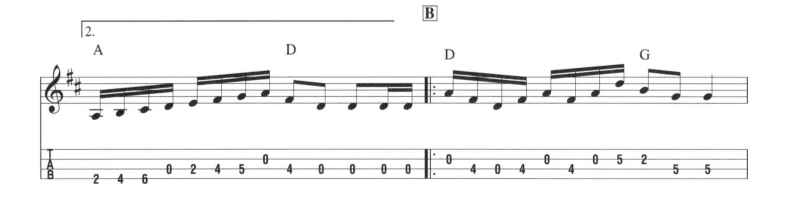

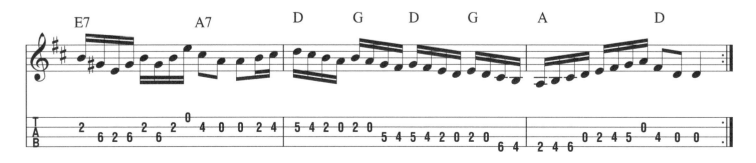

The [A] section is pretty straightforward in this bluegrass favorite, but the first two measures of the [B] section must be played with the marked picking in order to play this tune right.

WHISKEY BEFORE BREAKFAST

Traktik 19

Traditional

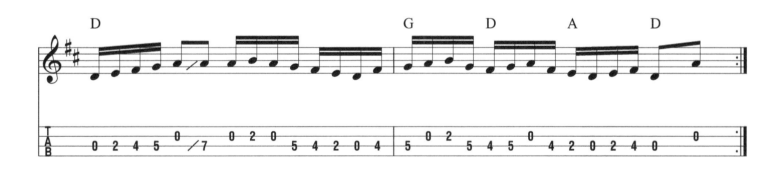

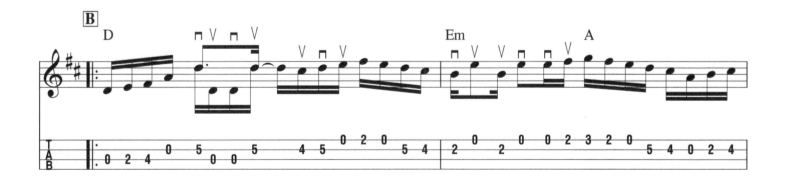

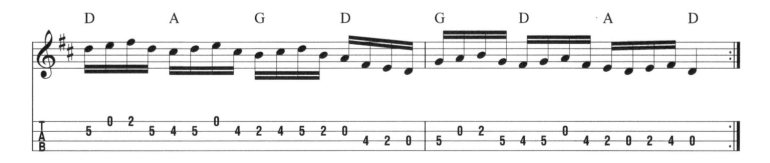

THE TUNES—KEY OF D

This song has a few good clichés that make it a good tune to learn when starting to play mandolin.

SOLDIER'S JOY

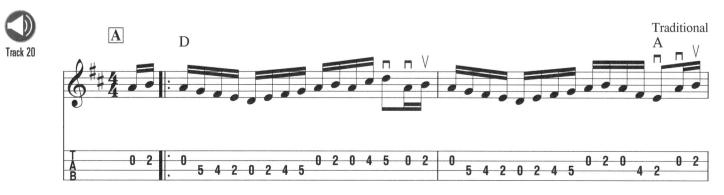

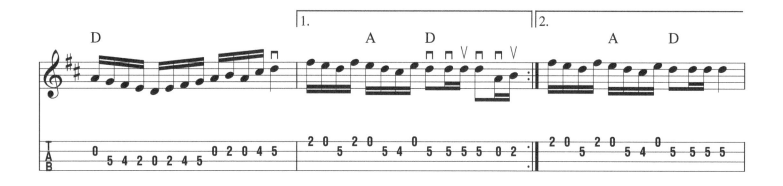

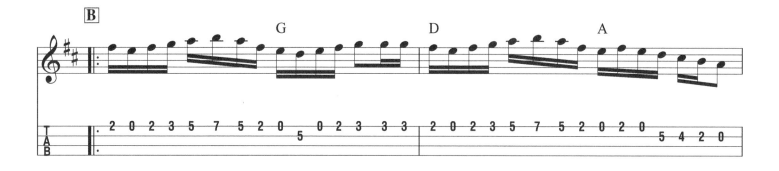

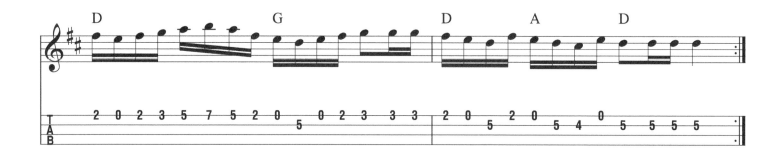

You may recognize this tune from Johnny Horton's 1960s hit "The Battle of New Orleans."

EIGHTH OF JANUARY

Traditional

Track 21

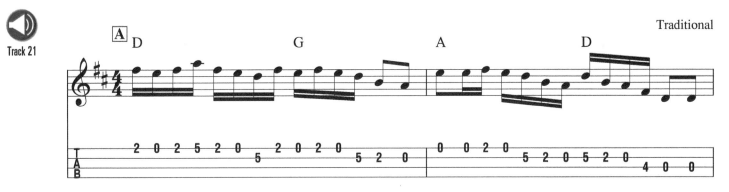

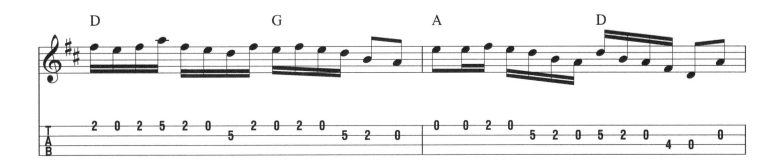

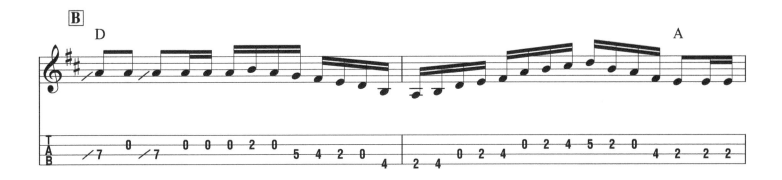

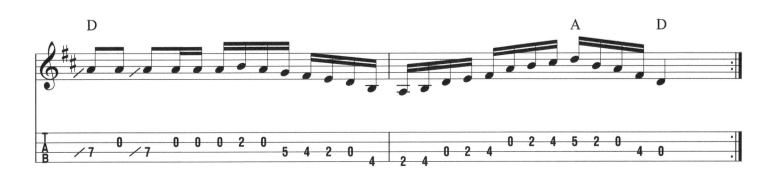

THE TUNES—KEY OF D

Ben Franklin is said to have wanted this tune to be our national anthem—or so the story goes. Make sure you play it as smooth as possible.

There is also an alternate Ⓐ section which is a bit more challenging but shows a an interesting use of arpeggios.

LIBERTY

Traditional

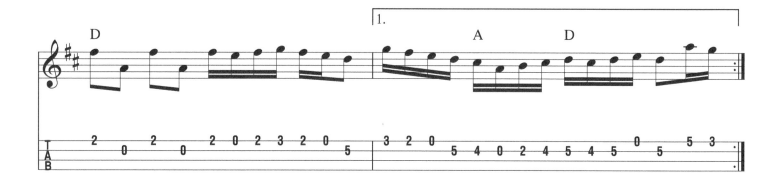

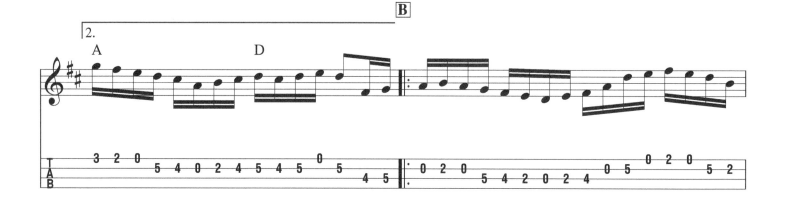

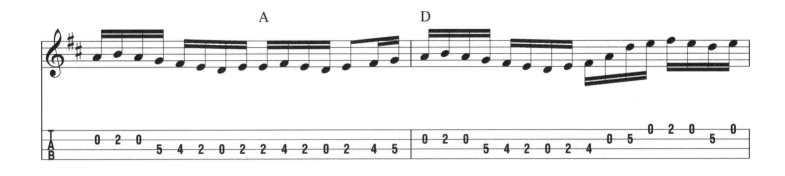

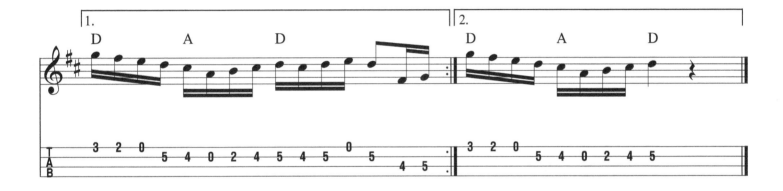

LIBERTY
ALTERNATE A SECTION

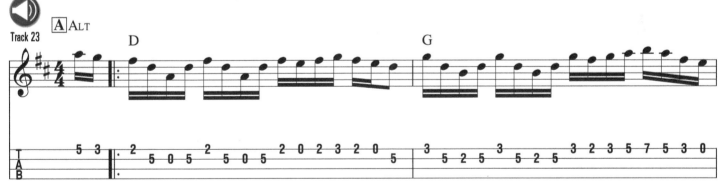

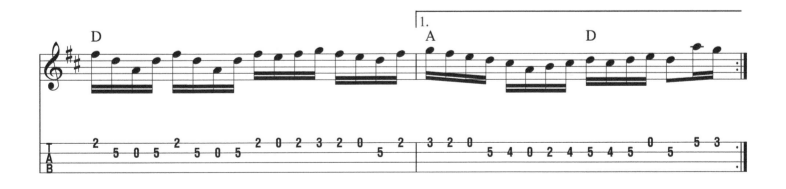

THE TUNES—KEY OF D

Start this tune with an upstroke and everything else will fall nicely into place. Also, use the proper pick direction on the slides in the [B] section.

FISHER'S HORNPIPE

Track 24

Traditional

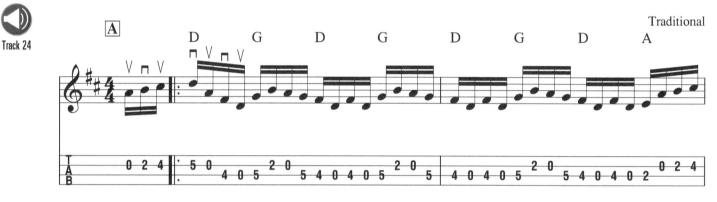

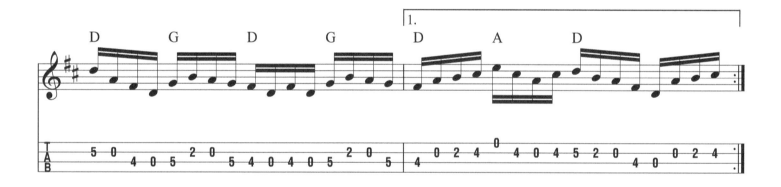

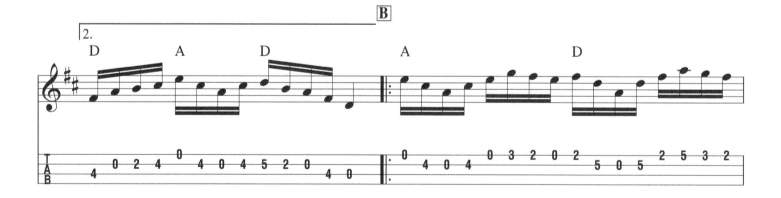

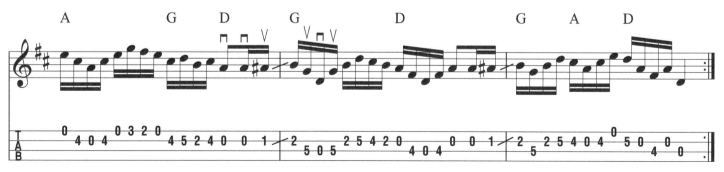

This is one of the great traditional American melodies, right up there with "Amazing Grace" and "Home Sweet Home."

Play the double stops at the beginning as if you were playing a fiddle, this will give it a classic old-time sound. Be sure to let the open string ring freely to get the right sound.

ARKANSAS TRAVELER

Track 25

Traditional

THE TUNES—KEY OF G

This song is one of the most-played fiddle tunes—it's important that you know this one. As always, watch the pick direction, especially in the B section.

Play the last two beats of the second measure of the B part with your second finger on the G.

BLACKBERRY BLOSSOM

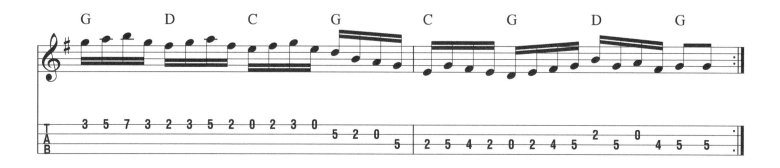

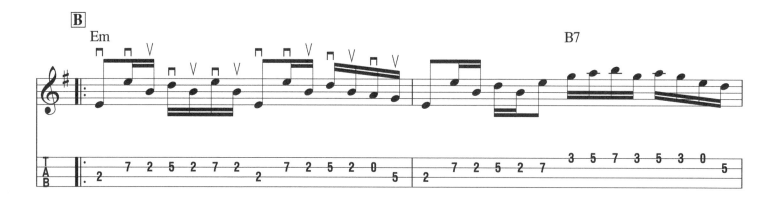

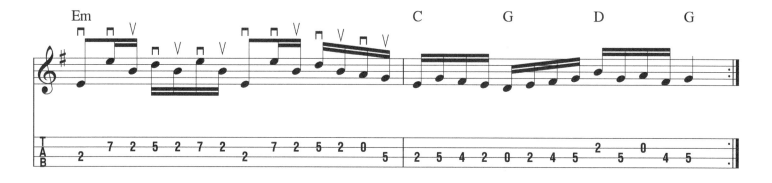

The B part of this song has double-stop fiddle shuffles. Use your index finger to bar the second fret in the fourth beat of the first measure.

On the third beat of the second measure of the B section, slide your third finger on the A string to get a cool slippery sound (listen to the recording); make sure you pick the double-stop fiddle shuffle nice and evenly to achieve this effect.

TEMPERANCE REEL

Traditional

Track 27

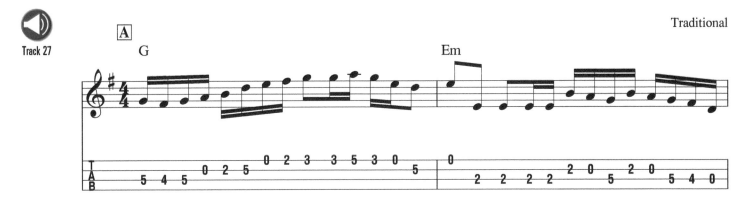

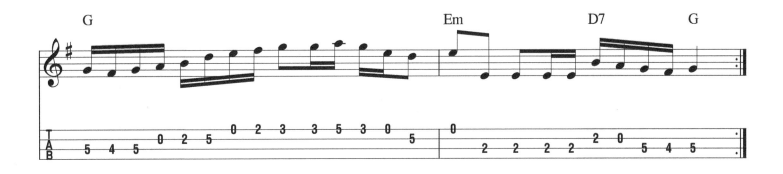

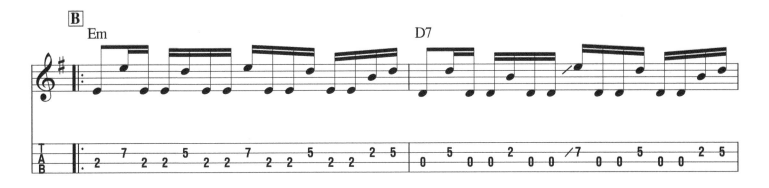

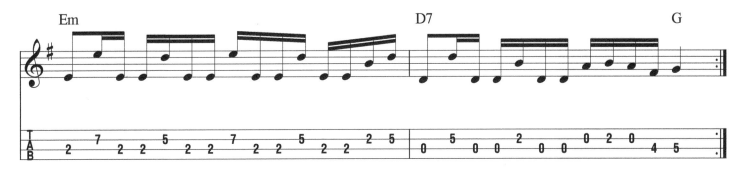

THE TUNES—KEY OF G

The first measure feels like it's being played backwards. Practice that part slowly for a while before moving on.

The double stops on section B can be tricky; isolate them and practice slowly until you can get them to sound clean.

TURKEY IN THE STRAW

Traditional

Track 28

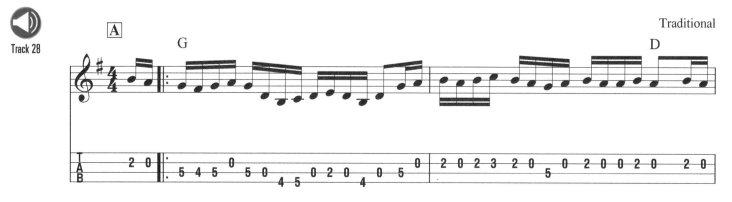

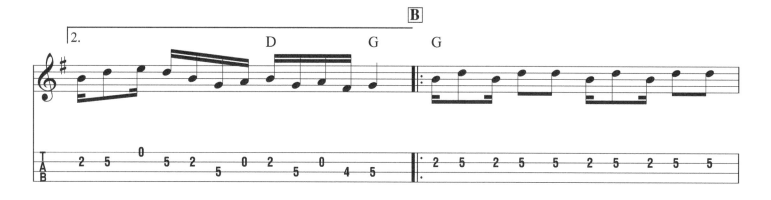

This classic Bill Monroe tune has a rock feel to it. Listen to the recording to get a good grasp of the phrasing.

Watch the picking marks when strumming the chords on the first and third measures of the B section.

KENTUCKY MANDOLIN

Bill Monroe

Track 29

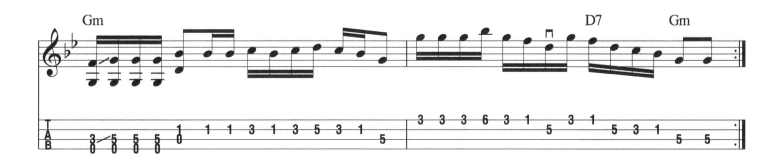

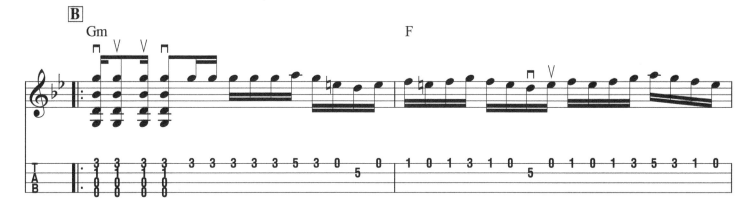

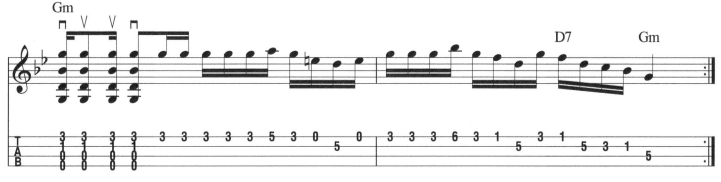

CONCLUSION

This collection of tunes should serve as a good starting point for mandolinists who are trying to build a solid repertoire, or as a reference for someone looking for new approaches and techniques for songs they already know. There is a balance between the basic arrangements of the tunes and interesting embellishments that would help mandolinists of all levels. I hope that you enjoy playing these tunes as much as I have over the years. Good luck!